C000170892

ROAD TRANSPORT
SOUTH EAST WALES

by Paul Heaton

P.M. Heaton Publishing
Abergavenny, Monmouthshire
Great Britain
2006

Front cover: Part of the Pritchards Transport fleet parked up at the weekend at their Polo Grounds Depot, at New Inn, Pontypool.
and
A Scania articulated outfit owned by Ellis Morgan & Son seen near Blackwood.

Back cover: A Volvo 8wl tipper of the Leyton Williams fleet shown at Brynmawr.
with
A Scania 6x4 tractor unit operated by Thomas Waste Management.
and
A Daf 6wl tipper owned by Alun Griffiths Contractors being loaded at Llanfoist.

Title page: A Canadian Dodge 4wl dropside tipper with sides removed owned by Cyril Williams of Brynmawr being loaded with a steel coil at Richard Thomas & Baldwin's Ebbw Vale Steelworks. It couldn't happen today, but it di c1949.

All rights reserved. Except for normal review purposes, no part of this book may be reproduced or utilised in any form or by any means, electrical or mechanical, including photocopying, recording or by any information storage or retrieval system, without written consent of the publishers and author.

ISBN 1 872006 22 1
© First Edition November, 2006

Published by P.M. Heaton Publishing,
Abergavenny, Monmouthshire, NP7 5EE

Printed in Great Britain by
The Amadeus Press,
Cleckheaton, West Yorkshire, BD19 4TQ

Typesetting by
Highlight Type Bureau Ltd, Bradford BD8 7BY

CONTENTS

A refuse collection vehicle operated by Royden Thomas's Abergavenny Waste Disposal making a collection in Market Street, Abergavenny, with the Town Hall in the background. He started undertaking this work – collecting trade waste, in the early 1980s at the request of the town's business people following a dispute with the council which saw them failing to make collections.

PREFACE

In this further volume on road transport I have featured businesses in South East Wales, two of which started out carrying on household removals before graduation into general haulage operating curtainside and van traffic. Another has been involved as civil engineers and road surface contractors for four decade operating a substantial fleet. Also covered is a major operator of modern eight-wheel tippers, and pionee in waste management. Finally a long since vanished business is included which was better known for it operation of steamers.

I am grateful to all those who have helped in the compilation of this book, including Bob Chivers, John Fletcher, Alun Griffiths, Derek Jones, Philip Morgan, Dario Passaro, John Pritchard, Mark Pritchard, Mrs Ann Reed, Mrs. Helen Thomas, Michael Thomas, Royden Thomas, Frank Whiting, Cyril Williams, Leyton Williams and Richard Williams.

I hope that, you the reader, enjoy this further volume on road transport.

Paul Heaton
Abergavenny
November 2006

Two modern units of the Leyton Williams fleet. Both Volvo FM12 8wl tippers, CN53DPX is finished in the Hanson blue colours whilst CN53 DTV sports the red livery of the Leyton Williams fleet.

ALUN GRIFFITHS CONTRACTORS, ABERGAVENNY

Visit Abergavenny today and you would be unable to miss the contribution made to the local economy by Alun Griffiths and his family. The origins of the businesses he founded go back almost four decades and he now operates a successful Civil Engineering and Road Surface Contracting firm based on Abergavenny with facilities at St. Clears in West Wales and at Machynlleth in Mid-Wales. The areas of operation are, however, spread over a far wider area including most of Wales, the South West and Midlands.

Born in the Rhondda on August 13, 1945, Alun Griffiths came to Abergavenny in 1964 where initially he was employed by the local construction company of Charlie Price and Son. In 1968 he went into business on his own account and by 1978 had acquired his own premises in the town. Checked on more than one occasion by recessions in the industry, he has nonetheless succeeded in expanding into becoming one of the biggest employers in the area.

In relation to the subject of this chapter – road transport, he operates a large fleet of tippers together with low-loaders, and it would be difficult to miss his huge fleet of grey and red liveried vans and pick-up trucks.

Think of road construction and civil engineering in Abergavenny and you think of Alun Griffiths.

General view of the Neville Street, Abergavenny yard showing plant and a Ford 4wl tipper of the Alun Griffiths fleet. THE BLORENGE mountain can be seen in the background.

Opposite top: Daf articulated tractor unit D858MCY operating with a low-loader semi-trailer.

Opposite bottom: When not operating as a low-loader, the Daf tractor unit D858MCY was coupled to this steel bodied tipping semi-trailer. This trailer was fitted with front end tipping gear. The dual use of this tractor unit enabled Alun Griffiths to make full use of the vehicle.

Above: I have been unable to find many photographs of the early fleet, hence this view of two vehicles at the end of their working lives. In the foreground is the accident damaged Leyland Bison 6wl tipper KHB54P and just in sight AEC Marshall 6wl tipper LAX515P.

Alun Griffiths operated a large fleet of tippers in the early days consisting of mostly Albion, Leyland and AEC 6 wheelers together with ERF and Volvo 8 wheelers DNY99V and DNY100V, one of which was entrusted to the late Albert Beyton.

This Daf 2300 6wl tipper G571HTH dating from 1981 is fitted with a steel rock body. This is a body without tailboard, where the floor at the rear is raised to ensure security of the load. Loaded, normally with large boulders it would not be practical to have a tailboard as it would be smashed when tipping such large and heavy single pieces of material. A number of the Griffiths vehicles are so fitted.

Above: G572HTH was a Leyland 6wl tipper.
Below: Another 6wl tipper is this steel bodied Daf – G573HTH.

This Mercedes 4wl tipper H610OUH was originally fitted with a conventional tailboard, but in the lower view tipping tarmac at the Angel Hotel, Abergavenny, is fitted with a two-piece door type tailboard.

Mercedes 4wl tipper H611OUH at the Neville Street Depot.

11

Pictured new, this Mercedes 6wl tipper H616OUH is seen at the Neville Street premises.

Above: This Mercedes 6 wheeler K887XWO is fitted with a 'rock' body.
Below: Leyland Daf 6wl tipper M362HTX operating from Abergavenny.

14

Opposite top: This Leyland Daf articulated tractor unit 250TUH operated as a low-loader for many years, and is pictured awaiting disposal having been replaced by a new Volvo FH12.

Opposite bottom: Small Leyland Daf tipper truck 143NNY seen at the Llanfoist facility.

Above: A view of a small part of the plant and equipment operated by Alun Griffiths Contractors.

Overleaf: Modern Daf 6wl tipper CN04EBZ being loaded.

Modern Daf 6wl tippers – CN06HJA, CN04EBZ and CN04EBX operated by Alun Griffiths Contractors.

This Volvo FM12 8wl flat CE02GZU with beavertail is fitted with a Palfinger hydraulic crane, making it an extreme useful piece of equipment.

Volvo FH12 6x2 tractor unit CN04AOK operates as a low-loader (Also pictured overleaf.)

Ellis Morgan & Son
OF PENGAM

*FURNITURE REMOVAL AND
HAULAGE CONTRACTORS*

LONG
DISTANCE
SPECIALISTS

ESTABLISHED
OVER
100 YEARS

Telephone: Pengam 330

Pwllglas House, Bryn Road, Blackwood, Mon., NP2 1LZ

ELLIS MORGAN & SON, BLACKWOOD

The well known haulage business trading as Ellis Morgan & Son with upwards of twenty vehicles can trace its origins back to 1820. In that year the business was founded at Pengam by Lewis Morgan, and with horse and cart served the farming community, carrying out whatever haulage needs were required in that area, including household removals. The second generation of the family Morgan Morgan was born in 1835 and by 1861 was described as 'carting agents for the Great Western Railway'. At that time young Morgan was 26 years old, and was living with his in-laws at Pencoed Cae Farm.

When a third generation of the family, again Morgan Morgan, took over the running of the business around 1900 it was established at Pwllglas Farm, Bryn Road, Pengam (Blackwood). Morgan married Mary Ann and their union was blessed with seven children – Charles (born 1905), Lucinda, Myfawwy, Violet, Ellis (who died in infancy), Ellis (born 1912) and Kathleen. Both Charles and Ellis, when they were old enough joined their father in the business still operating a horse and cart. Subsequently their mother Mary Ann Morgan took over the business herself, and a motor lorry was acquired for what had by then become almost exclusively household removals. They thereafter traded as M.A. Morgan, with both sons involved. Eventually Charles set up on his own account operating from a large site adjacent to the family home and yard at Pwllglas House. He became involved in goods vehicle sales, and vehicle parts, and became a substantial transport contractor in his own right operating in general haulage. Alas in 1990 he died without children.

In 1949 Ellis took over the removal business operating a single vehicle, and he was joined by his son Philip (born 1944) when he left school. Subsequently in 1963 a second vehicle was acquired and whilst maintaining their then core activity of household removals they entered general haulage transporting Dunlopillo products which being a light-weight payload was particularly suitable for their high cubic capacity vehicles. Further expansion was achieved when the Fibreglass factory was constructed at Pontyfelin, Cwmbran, and other high cubic loads were secured. This called for some articulated vehicles together with their traditional four wheelers.

Ellis retired in 1977 and the business passed to Philip and his sister Ann Nash Reed who carried on in partnership and continued to expand. In 1996 Philip's daughter Helen joined the firm where her husband Michael Thomas had been involved for six years. Expansion continued, with a loyal customer base, and in 2005 Michael and Helen took over the business. 2006 saw the connection with Pwllglas House end with the move to premises at Rogerstone, and nearer to their customer base. Rogerstone is particularly suitable with its direct access to the Motorway network.

The business continues to flourish, and the vehicles stand out in their traditional maroon livery. I recently undertook a journey towards London and counted six of their vehicles heading back towards South Wales – what a sight.

Pwllglas House, Bryn Road, Pengam – Base for the Morgan transport business for over a century. This view c1920 shows Morgan and Mary Ann Morgan with their family.

Morgan Morgan's horse and cart fitted out as a float c1908 showing a display by W. Morgan, Smith & Wheelwright, The Rock, Blackwood. Morgan Morgan seen holding his son Charlie clearly described as a haulage contractor and furniture remover of Blackwood.

Ellis Morgan (left), Charlie Morgan and Morgan Morgan seen with a Ford van, WO5752. This vehicle with an unladen weight of 1 ton 10¾ cwt was supplied new on October 30, 1931 by S.D. Roberts and Company, the Ford Depot, Pontllanfraith. By this time the business was actually being run by Morgan's wife Mary Ann Morgan, who traded as M.A. Morgan, Pengam.

Overleaf: This 1937 Bedford removal van, FXM560 was written off in a road accident in the Second World War. Ellis Morgan was returning home from London when an RAF vehicle carrying an aircraft with abnormal dimensions, unescorted and moving at night without authority was in collison. The Royal Air Force quickly took responsibility for the accident, and subsequently a large Dodge van was acquired as a replacement.

963 was an important year in the history of the business. Having always operated a single vehicle, in that year the eet was doubled in size. Two Austin vehicles are seen at Pwllglas House – the 1958 UWO497 and the new (1963) 13JWO. In 1949 Ellis Morgan had taken over the firm. He is shown with his son Philip, who marked the entry of fifth generation into the family venture.

Charlie Morgan became a substantial haulage contractor in his own right, and was also well known for his involvement in commercial vehicle sales and of spare parts. He operated from a site adjacent to Pwllglas House, and actually traded as Chas. Morgan.

Opposite top: This Thornycroft 4wl dropside was delivered new from the manufacturer's Basingstoke factory in 1955.

Opposite bottom: Charlie Morgan is seen taking delivery of this Albion articulated outfit 85HAX from Praills of Hereford in 1963.

Above left: This Atkinson 4wl dropside SAX10 was acquired new in 1958.

Above right: This Thornycroft 4wl dropside PAX10 was bought new in 1956.

Overleaf: Charlie Morgan is seen taking delivery of another Thornycroft, NWO685.

No challenge was too great for Charlie Morgan. He installed this footbridge at Gilfach, Bargoed, on the main Ystrad Mynach to Bargoed Road.

Opposite top: This 1963 Dodge 4wl flat 315JAX is laden with mineral water.

Opposite bottom: Charlie Morgan bought this Leyland 4wl flat DAX153C new in 1965.

Top left: Bedford Luton EAX440C.

Top right: This Seddon articulated outfit was laden with steelwork.

Above: This Dodge articulated outfit joined the Chas. Morgan fleet in 1969.

Above: A new Austin joins the Ellis Morgan fleet.

Left: This Bedford Marsden LED531P, shown at Pwllgla House arrived in 1976.

Opposite top: Ellis Morgan takes delivery of this Scania articulated outfit. Also shown Bob Penrose and Ron Counse of Scania. The vehicle is finished in the livery of customer Fibreglass.

Right: Philip Morgan is show with this Scania 92M, E961RK dating from 1988.

Part of the Ellis Morgan fleet seen in 1994, comprising articulated outfits – Scania 93M G667TWS, Volvo FH12 L226DAX, Scania 93 H561MDW and Mercedes 4 wheeler F366ATX.

Overleaf: The same vehicles in convoy near Blackwood.

Pages 46 & 47: This Scania 93M M69HNY is finished in the livery of a major customer.

pposite top: Mercedes tractor unit K924XWO *upled* to a York twin-axled van semi-trailer.

pposite bottom: Scania 114L tractor unit W253NTG *ith* a tri-axle curtainsider trailer.

Above top: Scania 4 wheeler CN53EZH with curtainsider body.

Above bottom: This Volvo FH12 tractor unit CN53DUU is seen at Pwllglas House.

Daf articulated tractor unit CE52WDL with her sister vehicle CE52WDJ just in sight on the left.

Above: The two Daf tractor units CE52WDL and CE52WDJ.

Left: CE52WDL having made a delivery for customer at Cologne.

PRITCHARDS TRANSPORT, PONTYPOOL

Cyril Charles Pritchard was born in 1918 and following war service was employed as a driver for the well-known Crickhowell firm of A.L. Watkins. In 1947 he established himself as a haulage contractor and acquired a Bedford 4wl dropside lorry with canvas awning. Most of his early work was devoted to household removals – the nearby Cwrt-y-Gollen Army Camp providing much work as married servicemen moved around the country. Thereafter he replaced this vehicle with an Austin supplied by Praills of Hereford, and subsequently a secondhand Bedford from Nash Motors, Cardiff, and then a new Ford from Praills.

In 1961, still operating from Crickhowell, he bought an Albion Claymore, with underslung engine and lengthened chassis allowing for a 20ft body. Thereafter he owned two Commer luton vans, the first of which came new from Moors in Cardiff. Cyril's son John joined him in the business in 1955 and expansion started into other work – mostly lightweight materials, and included pedal cycles from Falmanco at Pontnewynydd, work from Cooper's Mechanical Joints at Abergavenny, and Fibreglass at Pontyfelin, Cwmbran.

The first new articulated outfit, a Seddon arrived in 1972 from Praills of Hereford, and in 1982 it was decided to move to the Polo Grounds Industrial Estate, at New Inn, Pontypool, which was nearer and more convenient to most of their customer base. This coincided with John's son Mark joining him in the business. Considerable expansion was taking place and in 1987 the firm was incorporated as a limited company – Pritchards Transport Ltd. Subsequently John's daughter Debbie joined the business.

Today the firm operates a modern fleet of van bodied and curtainsider trailers and has a loyal customer base. Their modern fleet of upwards of twenty tractor units are liveried in outstanding clean white and blue colours. The success of this family owned and operated transport fleet is of great credit to them.

Pritchard's first articulated tractor unit, was this Seddon, MEU393L, delivered new in 1972 by Praills of Hereford. It marked a period of expansion by the business, which was still operating from Crickhowell.

Opposite top left: This Atkinson articulated tractor unit OHE702M fitted with a Gardner 180 engine was a useful vehicle.

Opposite top right: The Seddon Atklinson tractor unit CJ749S was supplied by Praills of Hereford.

Opposite bottom left: Scania 81 articulated tractor unit ORR933T.

Opposite bottom right: AVJ598V, a Seddon Atkinson was also supplied by Praills.

Above left: Scania 81 tractor, CHB276V, like most of the fleet was bought new.

Above right: Scania 82M, LDW219X, another new purchase.

Opposite top left: This Gardner-engined ERF 'B' series tractor unit OAX262X was supplied by South Wales Commercials, Newport.

Opposite top right: Another Gardner-engined vehicle was this 1980 ERF 'C' series tractor unit SUH476Y.

Opposite bottom left: John Pritchard is seen with this Seddon Atkinson tractor unit C539GHB which is finished in the livery of Pilkington's Insulation.

Opposite bottom right: Dating from 1986 is this Daf 2800 tractor unit.

Top: Atkinson OHE702M is seen at Crickhowell with the Seddon Atkinson KKG376W which is displaying the livery of customer Fibreglass Insulation.

Above: Another view of Seddon Atkinson KKG376W in the Fibreglass livery.

A view of the Crickhowell depot showing Seddon Atkinson, Atkinson and Scania tractor units.

A Seddon Atkinson and three Scania vehicles are shown at the Pritchard premises following the move to the Pole Grounds Industrial Estate, Pontypool.

Scania 4wl box van LDW214X in the days before full articulation of the fleet was achieved.

eddon Atkinson 4 wheeler AFO512V also fitted with a box van body. It emphasises the firm's clean white and blue
very.

This Daf 2800 articulated outfit D846KTX was travelling along the M4 Motorway eastbound towards the Severn Bridge on September 15, 1988, when it caught fire. Fortunately nobody was injured, but the modern vehicle was declared a write-off.

This ERF 'E' series (E10) tractor unit D274CDD was supplied new by Richard Read (Commercials) Ltd., Longhope, Gloucestershire.

ERF E10 – F277RDG with curtainsider trailer. The Pritchards had virtually standardised on the ERF marque for ov 20 years.

This ERF – H952RCL was an early example of the 6x2 configuration.

ERF 'E' series (E14), J541MDG shown at the Polo Grounds, Pontypool, depot.

pposite top: ERF 'E' series tractor unit K980SDD pauses at the entrance to the Polo Grounds premises.

pposite bottom: ERF EC11 tractor unit R633NDD with curtainsider semi-trailer.

bove: ERF 'E' series (EC14) M939JDW seen at New Inn, Pontypool.

ERF EC11 R632NDD is shown in the spacious and well equipped workshops at the Polo Grounds, New Inn, Pontypool.

Sister vehicle to the above, ERF – R633NDD.

Two ERF EC11 tractor units – 6x2 T881RDE and 4x2 V159UEW.

ERF EC11 6x2 tractor unit and curtainsider semi-trailer W746JNE.

Opposite top: ERF ECX 4x2 tractor unit X399AAD.

Opposite bottom: This ERF ECX 6x2 tractor unit Y183BOC is coupled to a tri-axled curtainsider semi-trailer.

Above: Although the Pritchard Transport fleet comprises of mostly ERF vehicles, there are a few Fodens, including this 6x2 tractor unit, CN03BZP.

Overleaf: Dockside view of ERF outfit NK51ZVS.

Noel Dando had just arrived at Pontypool from Dundee on May 21, 2006 with this Volvo FH12 articulated outfit, CN55 CBO.

Overleaf: part of the Pritchard Transport fleet shown at the weekend, comprising:
Foden CN04SNK
Daf XF CN06DWO
ERF ECX NK51ZVS
Foden 311XDE
ERF EC11 V139UEW
ERF ECX Y184BOC
ERF ECX Y183BOC
ERF ECX WU02JWO
ERF ECX Y59KJA
ERF EC11 W257WTU
Daf XF CN05FKK

THOMAS WASTE MANAGEMENT, BRYNMAWR

Royden John Thomas, born in 1944, set up in business in 1968 at Llangattock, Crickhowell, trading a Thomas Plant Hire but also operated tippers mainly on site work. He later operated from Gilwern and i 1981 from the Old Workhouse site in Abergavenny which coincided with his substantial entry into th skip hire business. At this time he was operating as Abergavenny Waste Disposal, and also starte collecting trade waste in and around the area.

In 1990 he entered into a joint venture trading as Abergavenny Waste Management, from the site at Ol Hafod Garage, Old Abergavenny Road, Brynmawr, which he had acquired two years earlier. In 1993 h set out again independently thereafter trading as Thomas Waste Management again from the Old Hafo Garage site.

Throughout his almost forty year career in business he has been joined by his wife Dianne, an subsequently by their four sons – Barry John, Howard Morgan, Clive Huw and Gareth Rhys – and thi family team continue to operate this thriving business in the waste disposal industry. A substantial flee of goods vehicles is operated together with modern plant.

In the upper views Royden Thomas's Ford tippe are involved in the reconstruction of th Monmouthshire and Brecon Canal where it ha been breached. Two of the tippers are LTG695 and RUH981M.

Opposite top: An early skip loader seen at the Ol Workhouse site at Abergavenny is this Bedford.

Opposite bottom: In the early 1980s Royde Thomas introduced the first private collections trade waste in Abergavenny. Whilst proper equipped refuse vehicles were bought for th purpose, initially a skip loader was used as show

76

Left & overleaf:
Abergavenny Waste Disposal refuse vehicle SBH954R is seen making a collection of trade waste in Market Street, Abergavenny.

A 'Family Business' – Royden and Dianne Thomas with their four sons, Barry, Howard, Clive and Gareth.

Abergavenny Waste Disposal's fleet of skip loaders.

This MAN skip loader was 'written off' in an outlying area of Crickhowell. A crane was used to recover the vehicle

Another view of the fleet of Abergavenny Waste Disposal at the Hafod Garage, Old Abergavenny Road, Brynmaw

82

Mercedes 8wl front loading waste collection vehicle.

Opposite top: Mercedes skip loader operating with a trailer, thereby increasing the overall capacity.

Opposite bottom: New Mercedes skip loader seen at Brynmawr.

Above: Refuse vehicle D262GOU used for trade waste collections.

Part of the Thomas Waste Management fleet seen at the Shepton Mallet Truck Show.

This Scania 124G 6x4 tractor unit S480AWP seen operating with a tri-axle ejector trailer.
In the lower view the vehicle is seen at the Silent Valley landfill site.

The Scania 6wl double drive tractor unit S480AWP operating as a low-loader.

Opposite top: Scania 8wl hook loader BF52JXO is a modern unit of the Thomas Waste Management fleet.

Opposite bottom: Mercedes skip loader R408DGU seen at Brynmawr.

Above: This Scania 6wl refuse vehicle is used for collections of trade waste.

WHITINGS TRANSPORT, LLANWENARTH CITRA

Three decades have elapsed since the transport business founded by Wilfred Whiting has disappeared. Hard to believe, but the location of this venture at Pantrhiwgoch Garage, Llanwenarth Citra, situated on the main A40 trunk road between Abergavenny and Crickhowell, was home to one of the biggest haulage fleets in the area.

Wilfred Whiting, was originally employed in the early 1920s as a driver with Tim Price, in the days when that business was operated from Llanover. This did not last long, as in 1923 he decided to go into business on his own account.

Expansion was dramatic, and within ten years he was operating upwards of ten vehicles. Early work consisted of bricks from the Beaufort Brickworks near Ebbw Vale, agricultural produce, including fertilizers and animal feedstuffs, and petrol and diesel-engined lorries, both dropside and tippers were in use. An important part of the business was the hourly-rate hire of vehicles to Brecknockshire County Council, and the eventual hire of tractors fitted with front loading shovels, both used in road repairs and resurfacing.

However, it is the use of Sentinel Steam wagons that Whitings are best remembered for. He owned a number of these vehicles, in the early days being fitted with solid tyres, and eventually with pneumatic tyres. These were the true heavy-weights of their era, and were still being acquired new even as late as the mid-1930s.

Prior to the Second World War, he had a number of Foden 6wl dropsides, and some of the work for these vehicles saw them loading at the goods sidings at Abergavenny, for distribution throughout South East Wales. Most of these Fodens were requisitioned for the military during the war, never to return.

Always a well-turned out fleet, they were painted in a dark brown livery.

After the war whilst maintaining hitherto core activities, much steel traffic was undertaken usually from Richard Thomas & Baldwin's Ebbw Vale Steelworks, and by 1962 a huge fleet entered service on contract to and in the colours of RTB. Whilst Atkinson, AEC 8wl and Dodge 6wl dropside flats were being used, the major part of the operation centred on Dodge and ERF articulated tractor units coupled to 4-in-line semi-trailers.

In the late 1960s the contract at Ebbw Vale passed to others, and the blue vehicles and trailers were disposed of. The vehicles with Special 'A' licences continued, comprising Dodge 6wl and articulated outfits. The business diversified, and by this time his son Frank was involved in its direction. However I do recall a brand new Bedford KM tipper appearing in the familiar Whiting-colours in 1972, this being KEU137K, although haulage was soon given up. Yet another of Monmouthshire's old established transport fleets had disappeared.

DELIVERY NOTE

Nº 03910

TELEPHONES 421 AND 422

WHITING'S TRANSPORT LTD
LLANWENARTH GARAGE, Nr. CRICKHOWELL

M..19........

Lorry No................. Driver's Name...

Please Receive:

Customer's Signature..

Although going into business in 1923 Wilfred Whiting had a partner for a short period, and at first traded as Hawkins & Whiting. This early Sentinel DG8 8wl dropside with solid tyres was lent to him by the Shrewsbury manufacturer in order to let him earn the deposit for a new vehicle. It was in connection with steamers that Whitings are best remembered for.

This 6wl Sentinel steam waggon was involved in an accident, finishing up on its side in a field. The location believed to be near Builth Wells.

This Sentinel 8wl S8 steam waggon WO8854 entered the Whiting fleet on October 6, 1934. It is seen carrying bricks for the Ebbw Vale Company.

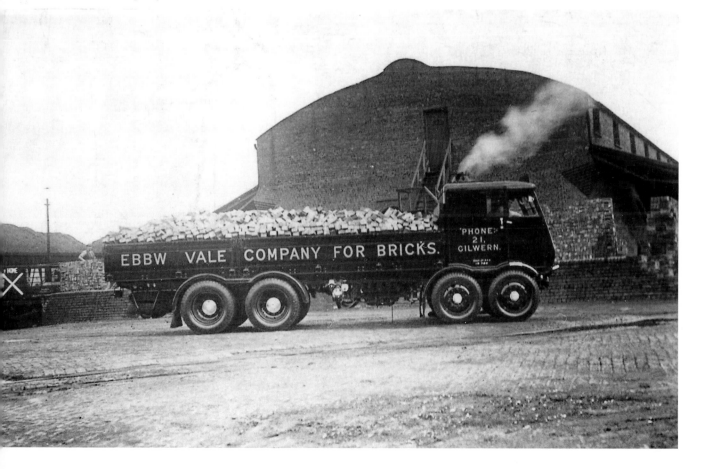

This Sentinel 4wl steam waggon was badly damaged in an accident at the junction of Park Crescent and Herefor Road, Abergavenny.

Above and opposite: These Foden 6wl vehicles were an important part of the immediate post-war fleet.

Opposite top: Three Dodge 4wl tippers seen at Pantrhiwgoch Garage, Llanwenarth Citra in the 1950s. From the left RAX59 – Jim Ploughman, OWO747 – Jack Dando, and OWO296 – Ike Jones.

Opposite bottom: Dodge tipper RAX59.

Above: Another Dodge tipper at Llanwenarth Citra.

Overleaf: Units of the Whitings fleet employed in the relining of a coke oven at Richard Thomas & Baldwin's Ebbw Vale Steelworks in 1957.

Bedford OWLD dropside at Llanwenarth Citra.

Bedford 4wl dropside KAX774 dating from 1952.

Jack Dando (left) and Tyrone Brown having just finished loading the Bedford LWO308 with bricks.

Albion 6wl flat loaded with tinplate from Ebbw Vale steelworks.

In the early 1960s Whitings Transport Ltd were awarded a major contract by Richard Thomas & Baldwin Ltd., Ebbw Vale. This marked the introduction of articulation into the works and indeed the Whitings fleet. This group of seven Dodge tractor units with single axle coil semi-trailers were the first vehicles acquired for the contract. They were finished in the RTB light blue livery and are shown at the Pantrhiwgoch Garage at Llanwenarth Citra, situated on the A40 road between Abergavenny and Crickhowell.

STEEL SPECIAL

FEATURED at the Commercial Motor Show at Earls Court recently was this vehicle painted in the light blue RTB livery. Shown on the British Trailer Company's stand, the vehicle is owned by Whiting's Transport Ltd. of Crickowell and is used by Ebbw Vale under contract.

The tractor and trailer; both of the latest type, is due to go into service with the Company shortly. The heavy duty ERF tractor is fitted with a Gardner 150 engine with overdrive and double reduction hub and is capable of pulling a total weight of 28 tons.

The semi-trailer was specially built by the British Trailer Company and has Four-in-Line running gear with oscillating axles.

A 26 ft. coil well enables the trailer to carry anything from a 15 ton coil to a full load of smaller coils. Specially slotted coil wedges support coils when carried, or can be used as additional chock rails when carrying flat steel.

When carrying coils, the well covers are carried in a special underslung container.

On return journeys from delivering steel, the vehicle will carry materials for the Works.

The expansion of the contract at Richard Thomas & Baldwins Ebbw Vale steelworks saw the acquisition of number of ERF LV tractor units and BTC 4-in-line trailers. This particular vehicle was featured at the Commerci Motor Show in 1964.

This Dodge 6wl flat WAB835 operating on an 'A' licence retained the Whitings brown livery.

After withdrawing from road transport in the early 1970s, the Whitings family operated a successful caravan sales and service business at the Llanwenarth Citra site, trading for a number of decades as Crickhowell Caravans.

LEYTON WILLIAMS, BRYNMAWR

Born in 1950 Leyton Williams, on leaving school undertook an apprenticeship as a boilermaker a Richard Thomas and Baldwin's Ebbw Vale steelworks. On completion at 20 he entered road haulage on his own account, and bought a Bedford TK tipper. With this vehicle he operated out of local quarries and on daywork. Thereafter he owned a couple of Ford D800 tippers, and by 1980 was working for the coal board hauling shale from washeries, coal from opencast sites and aggregates from local quarries. Most of his work is based in South Wales, and for a time he owned a skip hire business, but also hauled waste from various sites in South Wales.

In 1987 he bought his first eight-wheeler, and ran a number of Leyland Constructor tippers. In 1990 he purchased his first Volvo 8wl tipper, and now operates a substantial fleet of modern Volvo and Scania vehicles. His policy is to buy new and replace when three years old. This has the effect of vehicles holding a good resale value and with maintenance contracts with manufacturers holds down operating costs. This is witnessed by seeing just how modern his substantial fleet is – a credit to his vision and enterprise.

Operating out of Brynmawr; in 2006 he has established a waste transfer facility, and has re-entered the skip hire business. In 1987 he was joined in the business by his son Richard, and they now operate successfully as Leyton Williams Haulage Ltd.

This Volvo FL7 6wl tipper F806TPR is seen hauling out of a local quarry.

Early 8-wheelers in the Leyton Williams fleet comprised a number of these Leyland Constructors fitted with a bulk body.

Above & overleaf on page 110: Leyton's son Richard drove this Mercedes 4wl tipper from new.

Richard's first 8-wheeler was this Volvo FL10 – L215DAX.

Three Volvo FL10 8wl tippers, P96BFO, M907HDW and L215DAX.

Another view of Volvo P96BFO.

Leyton William's first Volvo FL12, R383BTX loading ex-quarry.

Another view of R383BTX.

Four units of the Leyton William's fleet operating for MAFF, Y699GBO, R383BTX, X959CAX and T597VAX.

Such is the policy of this Brynmawr based business, that this line of six relatively modern Volvo 8-wheelers hav already been replaced in the fleet with new vehicles.

A modern unit of the fleet seen tipping.

T597VAX with a country backdrop.

Volvo FM12 – CN51KZB seen at Brynmawr.

This Scania 8wl tipper CE02GKX was the first vehicle from this manufacturer.

Whilst the Leyton Williams livery is red, this Volvo CN53DPX is finished in Hanson's blue colours.

CN53DTV is about to refuel at Brynmawr.

This pair of Scania 8wl tippers were not placed in service straight away when purchased, thus their '05' registration numbers had to be re-allocated as '06'.

New Scania 8wl tipper CN06EEP refuelling at Brynmawr.

P.M. HEATON PUBLISHING

Paul Heaton was born at New Inn, Pontypool, in 1944 and was educated at Greenlawn Junior School in New Inn and the Wern Secondary School at Sebastopol. At fifteen he commenced employment, at first in a local store and then with a builders' merchant. A year later he was appointed as a Deck Cadet in the Merchant Navy, with the Lamport & Holt Line of Liverpool, and served in their vessels *Chatham*, *Constable* and *Romney* usually in the Brazil and River Plates trades. he joined the Monmouthshire Constabulary (now Gwent) in 1963, and served at Abergavenny, Cwmbran, Newport, the Traffic Department, the Motor Cycle Section, as the Press Liaison Officer, and for five years represented Inspectors for the whole of Wales nationally on the Joint Central Committee of the Police Federation. he was promoted to sergeant in 1974 and Inspector in 1982. On his retirement he served as Market Inspector with the RSPCA for eight years and at the same time was Landlord of a Public House for three years.

He has always maintained an interest in maritime history and in transport generally, and for a period of ten years had numerous articles published in the magazine *Sea Breezes*. He has had the following books published:

Reardon Smith 1905-1980 (1980)
The Baron Glanely of St. Fagans and W.J. Tatem Ltd., with H.S. Appleyard (1980)
The 'Redbrook', A Deep-Sea Tramp (1981) four editions
The 'Usk' Ships (1982) two editions
The Abbey Line (1983)
Kaye, Son & Co. Ltd., with K. O'Donoghue (1983)
Reardon Smith Line (1984) two editions
The South American Saint Line (1985)
Welsh Blockade Runners in the Spanish Civil War (1985)
Lamport & Holt (1986) two editions
Tatems of Cardiff (1987)
Booth Line (1987)
Jack Billmeir, Merchant Shipowner (1989)
Welsh Shipping, Forgotten Fleets (1989)
The Gallant Ship 'Stephen Hopkins', with R.J. Witt (1990)
Palm Line, with Laurence Dunn (1994)
Not All Coppers Are ...! (1994)
Wynns – The First 100 Years for John Wynn (1995) three editions
Wynns – The Last 20 Years for John Wynn (1996)
L.C. Lewis, Heavy Haulage (1996)
Wynns Overseas first draft for John Wynn (1998)
The Wynns Fleet – 120 Years of Road Haulage (2003)
Lamport & Holt Line (2004)
Road Transport Gwent (2004)
Road Transport Monmouthshire (2005)
Road Transport Wales & Border (2005)
Spanish Civil War Blockage Runners (2006
Road Transport South East Wales (2006)